DC SUPER HEROES

THE SCIENCE BEHIND SUPERMAN'S™ SPEED

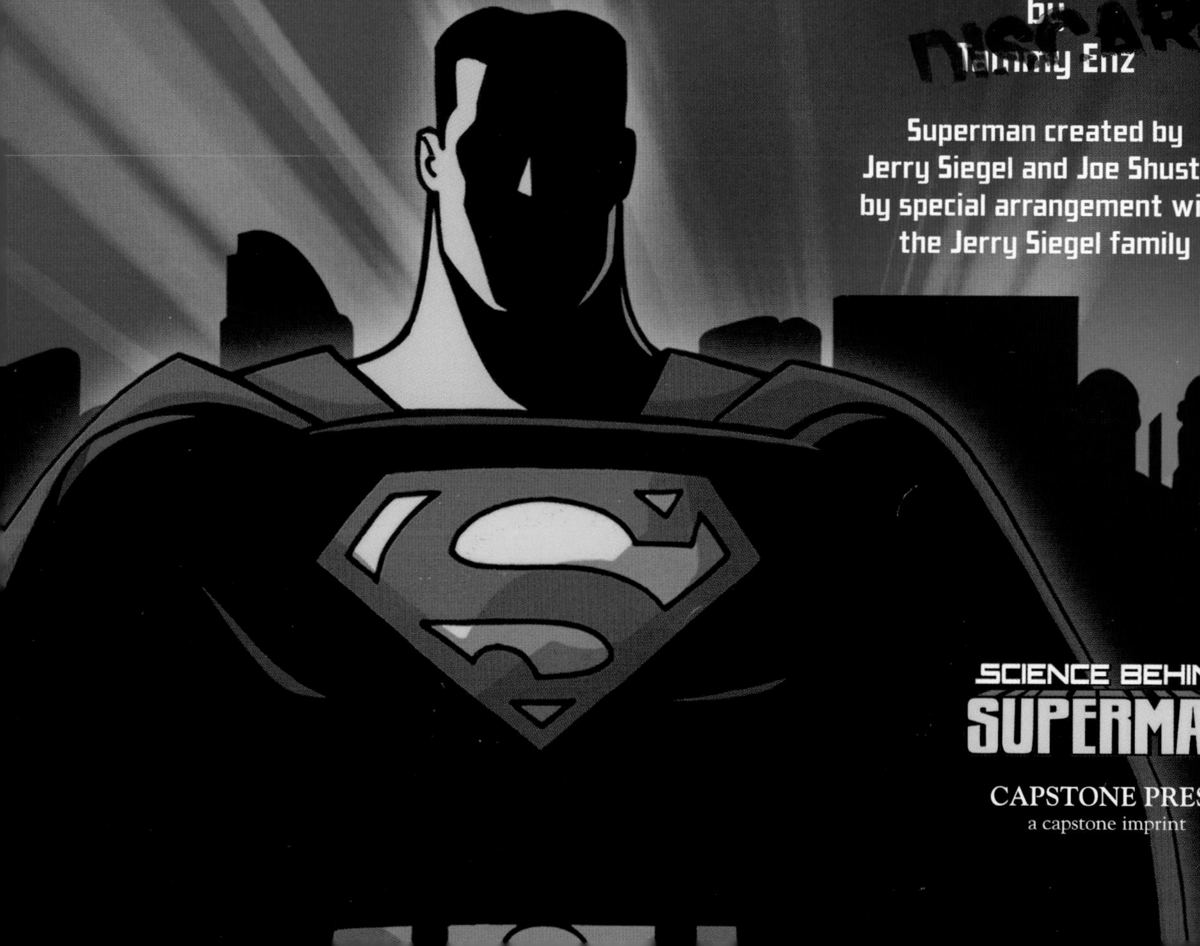

by
Tammy Enz

Superman created by
Jerry Siegel and Joe Shuster
by special arrangement with
the Jerry Siegel family

SCIENCE BEHIND SUPERMAN™

CAPSTONE PRESS
a capstone imprint

Published by Capstone Press in 2017
A Capstone Imprint
1710 Roe Crest Drive
North Mankato, Minnesota 56003
www.mycapstone.com

STAR38176

Library of Congress Cataloging-in-Publication Data
Names: Enz, Tammy, author.
Title: The science behind Superman's speed / by Tammy Enz.
Description: North Mankato, Minnesota : Capstone Press, 2016. | Series: DC super heroes.
  Science behind Superman | Audience: Ages 7-9. | Audience: K to grade 3. | Includes bibliographical
  references and index.
Identifiers: LCCN 2016033217 (print) | LCCN 2016040733 (ebook) | ISBN 9781515750963 (library binding) |
  ISBN 9781515751007 (paperback) | ISBN 9781515751120 (eBook PDF)
Subjects: LCSH: Speed—Juvenile literature. | Kinematics—Juvenile literature. | Superman (Fictitious character)—
  Juvenile literature.
Classification: LCC QC137.52 .E594 2016 (print) | LCC QC137.52 (ebook) | DDC 531/.112—dc23
LC record available at https://lccn.loc.gov/2016033217

Summary
Explores the science behind Superman's speed and describes examples of speed from the real world.

Editorial Credits
Aaron Sautter, editor; Veronica Scott, designer; Kelly Garvin, media researcher;
Katy LaVigne, production specialist

Photo Credits
Alamy/Chris Batson, 9; Capstone Press: Erik Doescher, backcover, 1, 3, 6, Ethen Beavers, 17, 21, Luciano Vecchio, 8, 10, Mike Cavallaro, cover, Min Sung Ku, 4, 22, Rick Burchett/Lee Loughridge, 5; Minden Pictures/Robert Valentic, 15; Newscom: Everett Collection, 19, Hennessey/Splash News, 18; Shutterstock: muratart, 13, Steve Oehlenschlager, 16, Triff, 7, Vadim Sadovski, 11, 20, Volt Collection, 14

Printed and bound in the USA.
010023S17

Table of Contents

MAR   2017

SPEED SAVES THE DAY

Wherever criminals strike, Superman is fast enough to save the day. He can outrun bullets and zip around the globe in a few seconds. Nothing comes close to Superman's incredible speed. But some real world things may challenge even the Man of Steel's power of speed.

FACT

Superman first appeared in *Action Comics* #1 in 1938.

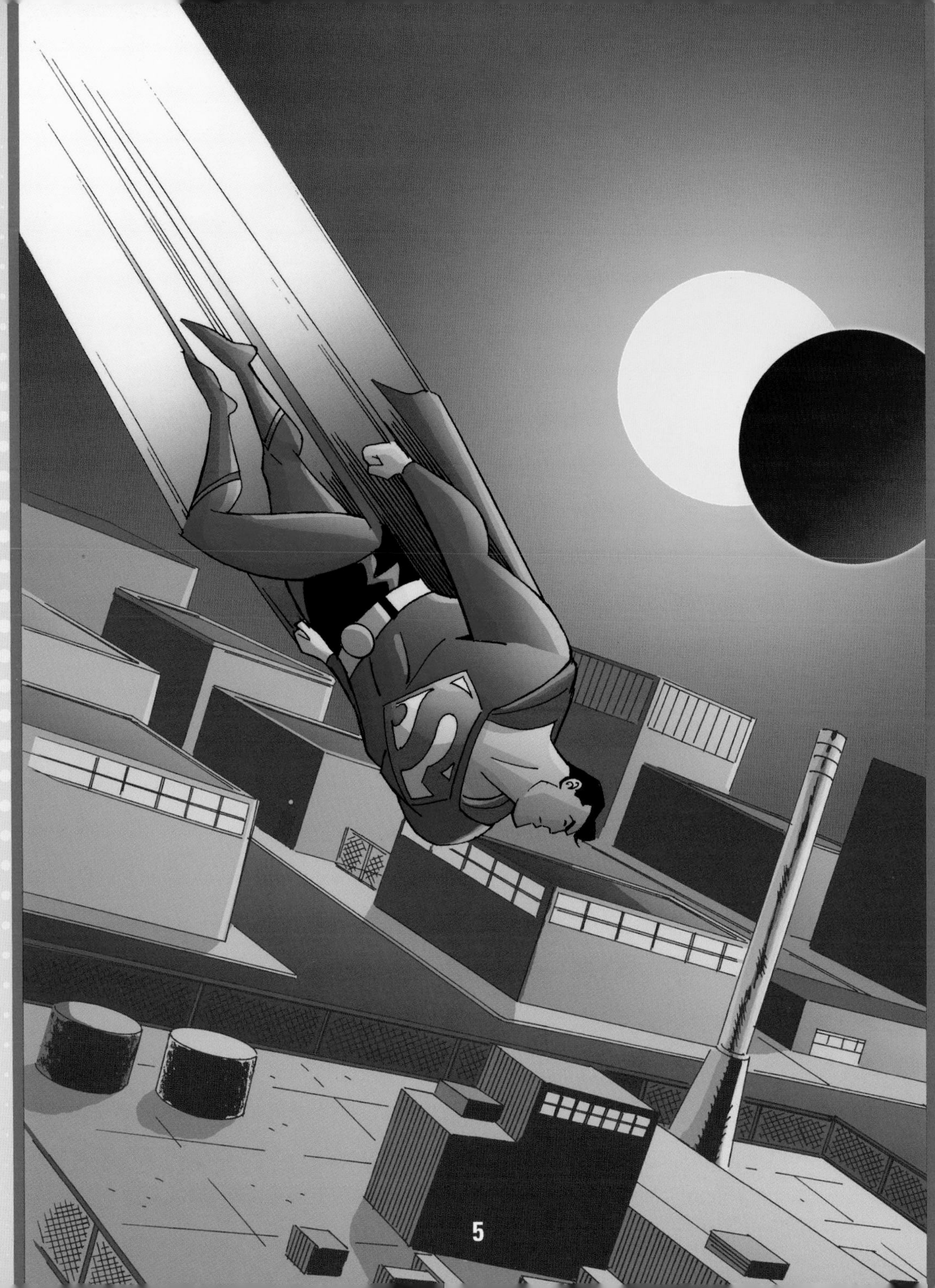

CHAPTER 1

UNDERSTANDING SPEED

Speed is critical for Superman to stay ahead of criminals. But what is speed? Simply put, speed is a measure of the distance an object travels in a certain amount of time. All moving objects have speed. Even a slow-moving snail has speed. It just doesn't have as much as a race car or rocket.

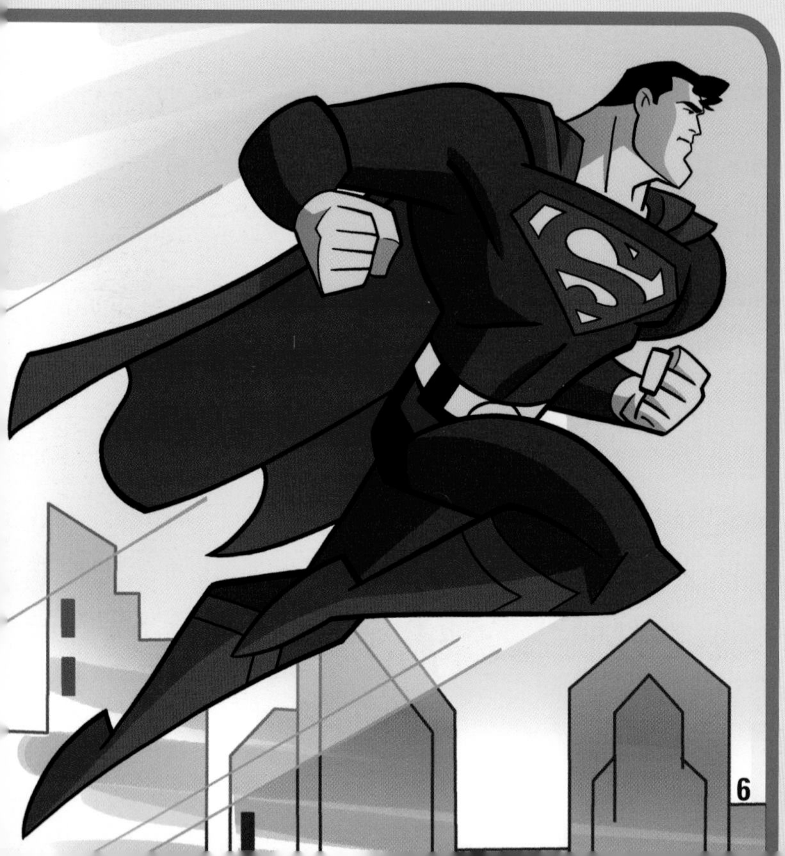

FACT

Right now, you are traveling faster than Superman! The Earth **orbits** around the Sun at about 67,000 miles (107,800 kilometers) per hour. Now that's fast!

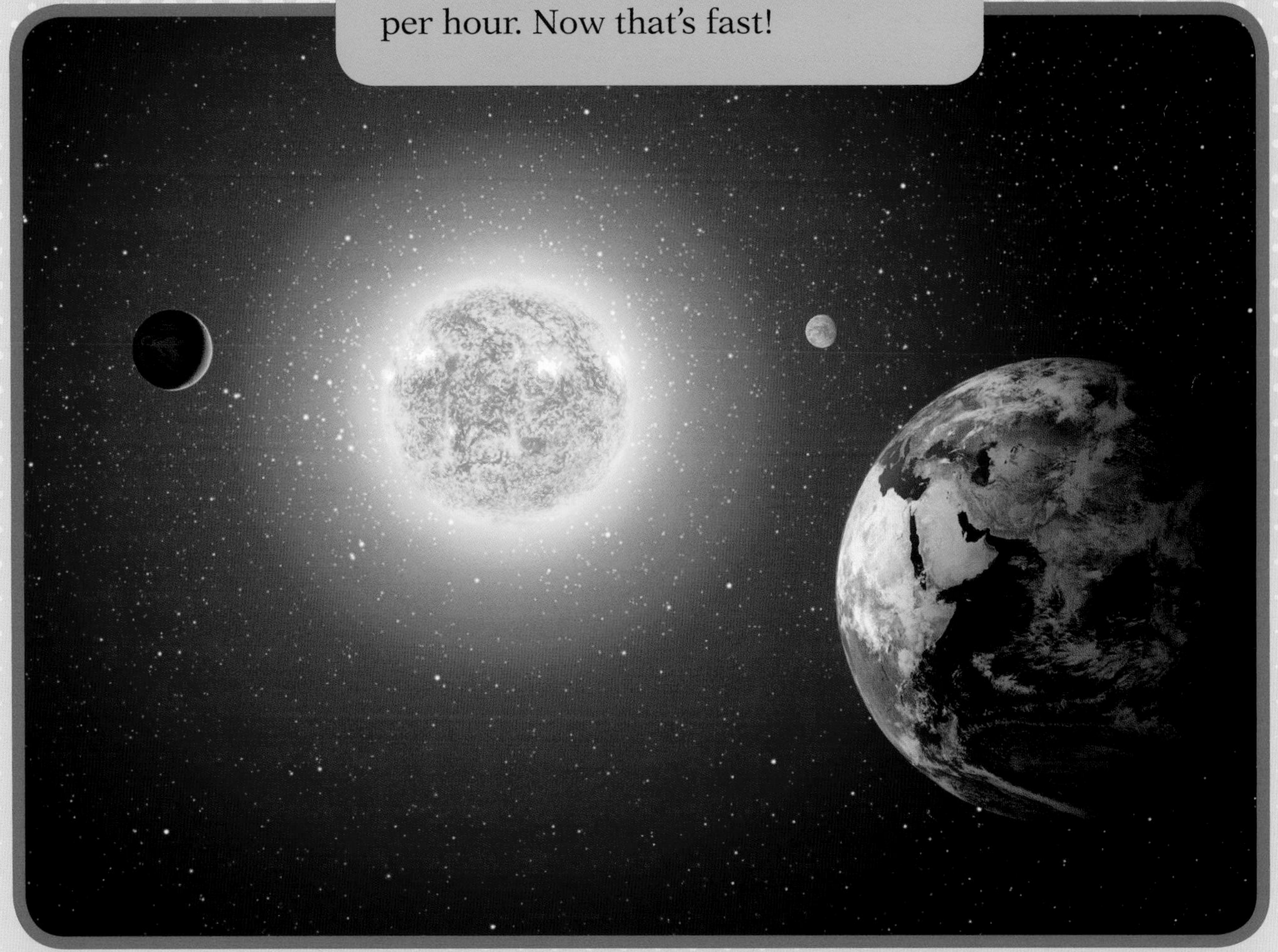

orbit—to travel around an object in space

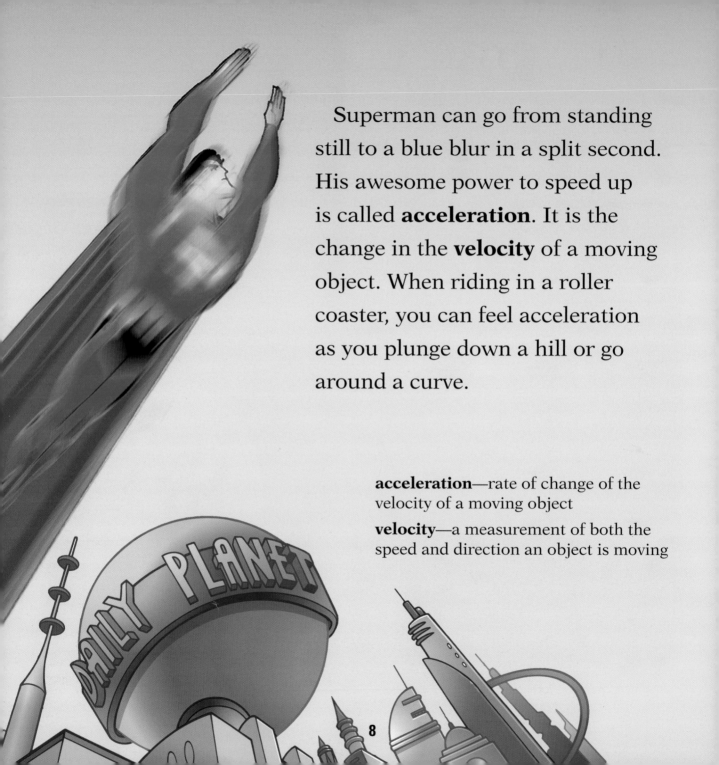

Superman can go from standing still to a blue blur in a split second. His awesome power to speed up is called **acceleration**. It is the change in the **velocity** of a moving object. When riding in a roller coaster, you can feel acceleration as you plunge down a hill or go around a curve.

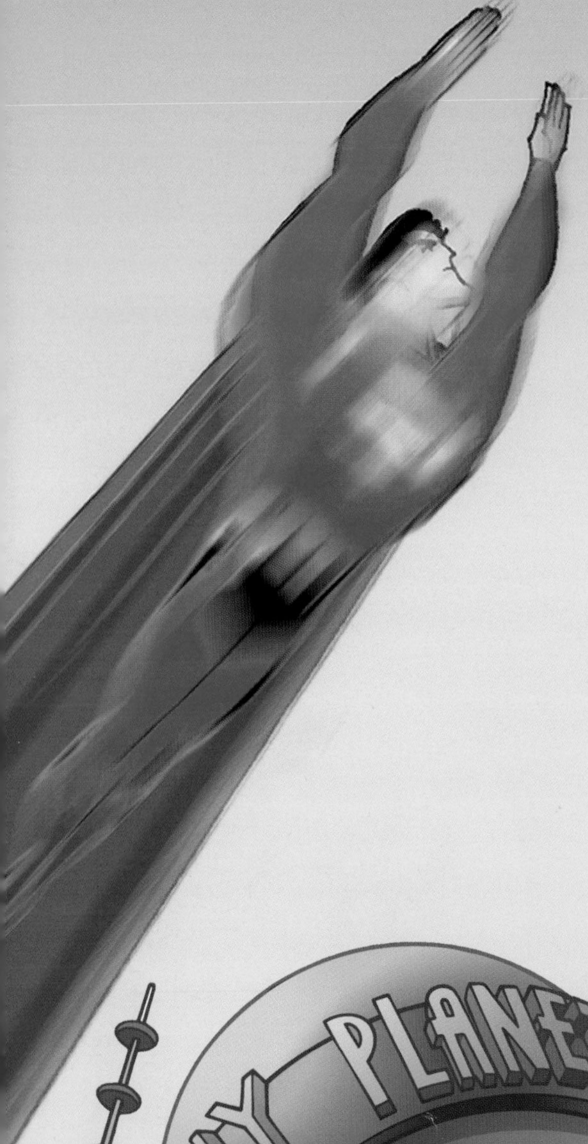

acceleration—rate of change of the velocity of a moving object

velocity—a measurement of both the speed and direction an object is moving

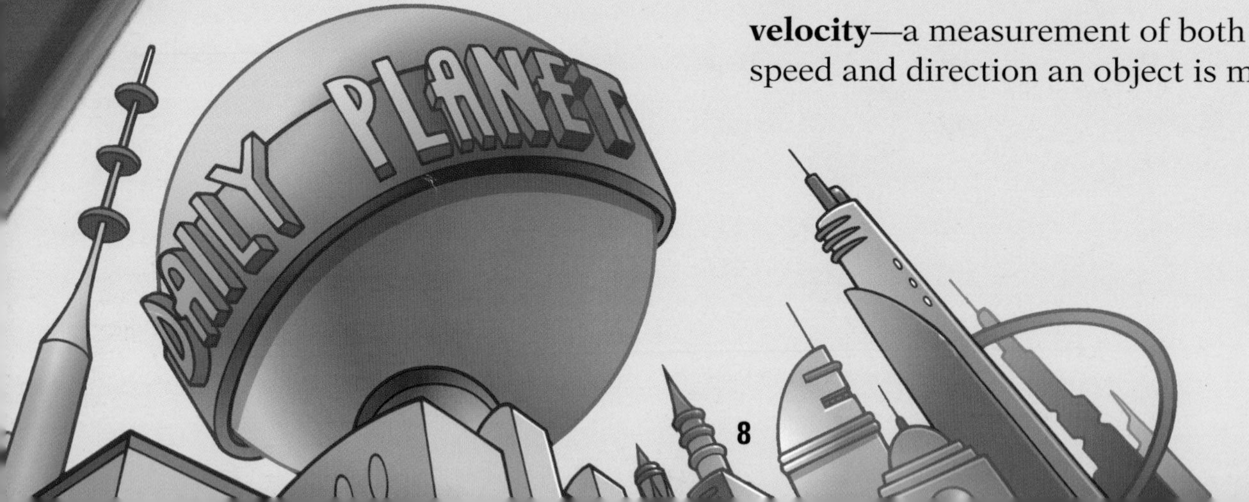
DAILY PLANET

FACT

Formula Rossa is the world's fastest roller coaster. It accelerates from zero to 62 miles (100 km) per hour in just two seconds!

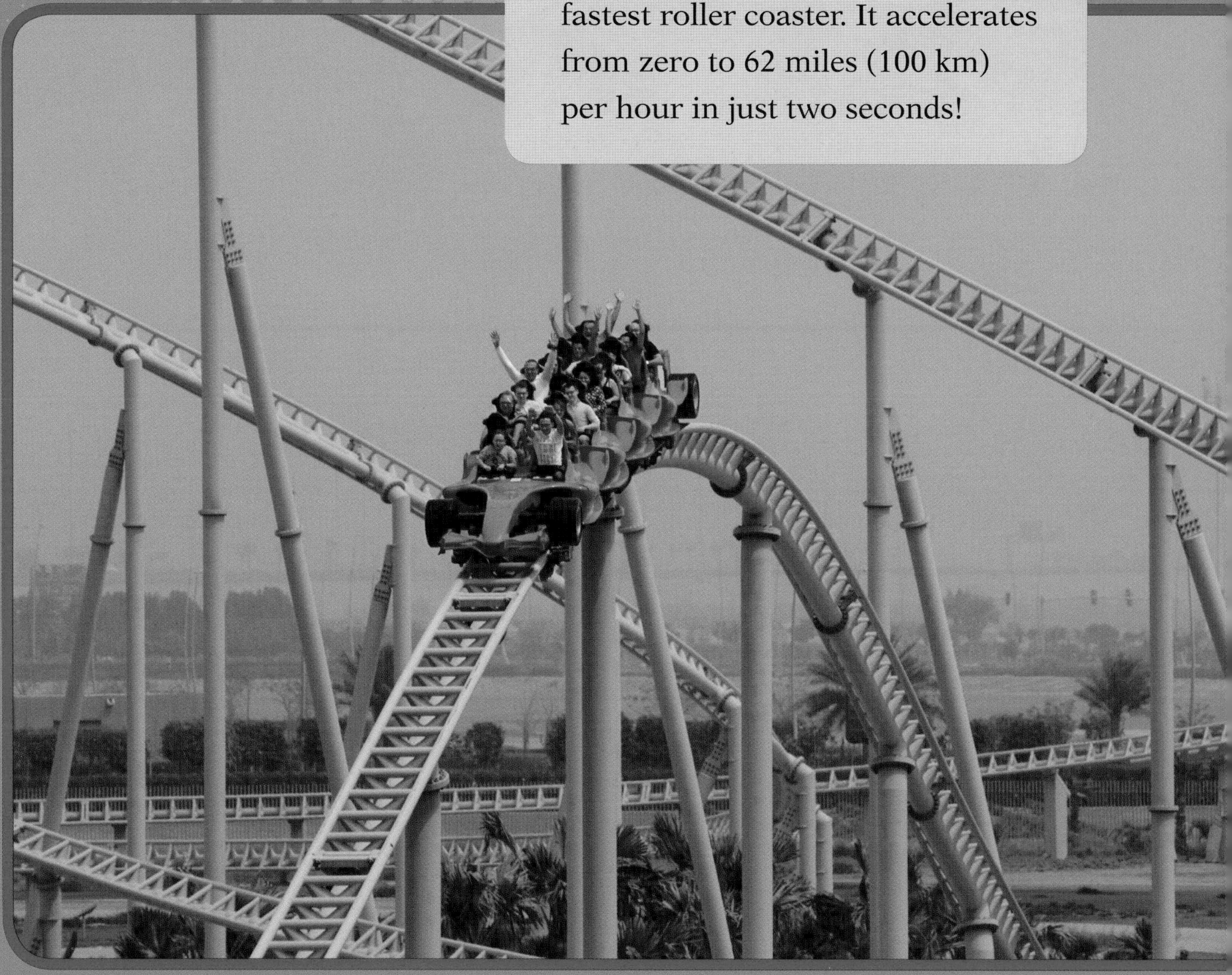

Superman sometimes flies faster than the speed of sound. **Sound waves** travel through the air at 761 miles (1,225 km) per hour. But that's nothing compared to the speed of light. Light travels at 186,000 miles (299,300 km) per second. In one year, a beam of light can travel 6 trillion miles (9 trillion km)!

sound wave—a wave or vibration that travels through a substance, such as air

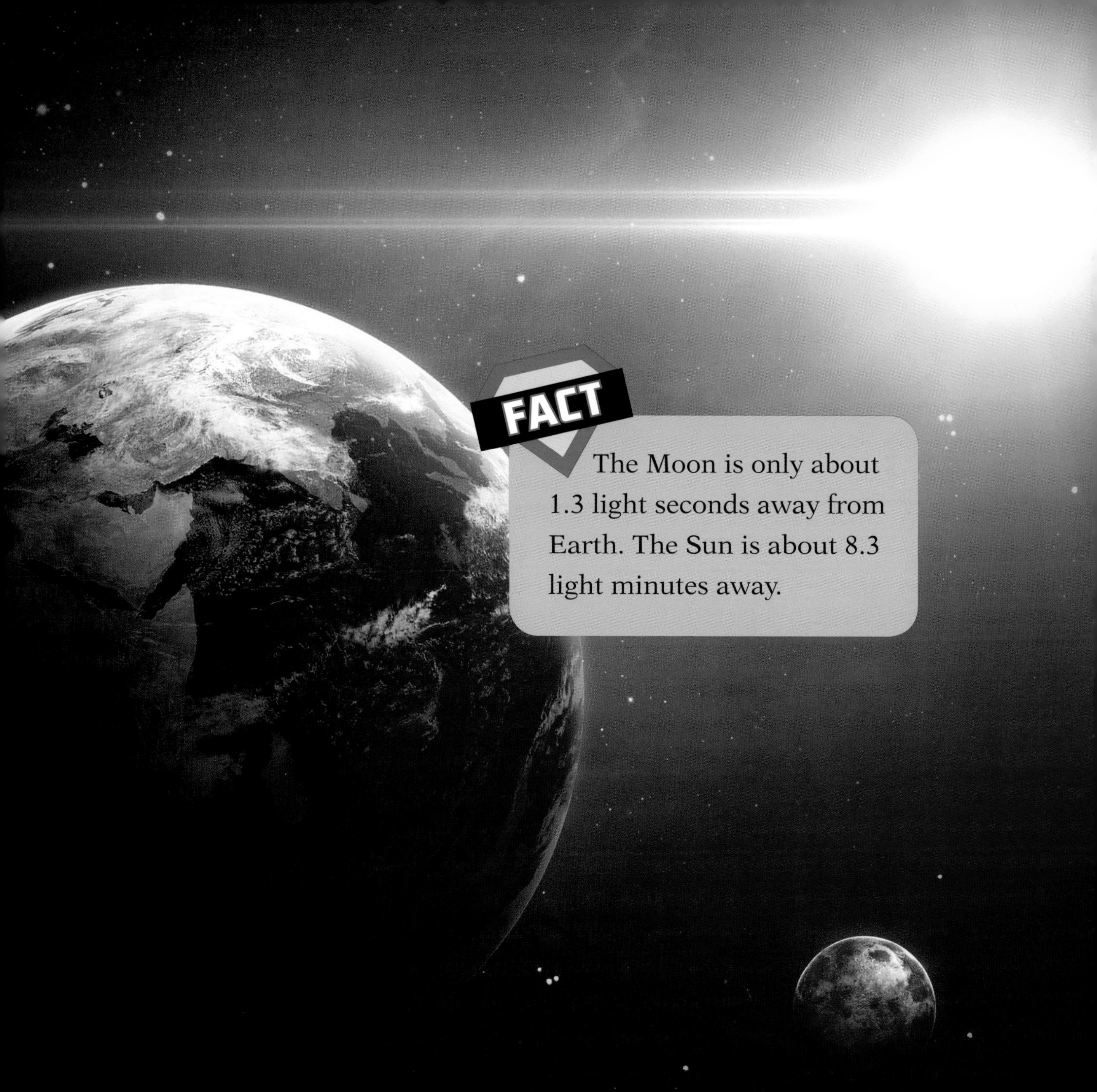

FACT

The Moon is only about 1.3 light seconds away from Earth. The Sun is about 8.3 light minutes away.

Gravity and friction are the enemies of speed. Gravity pulls all things toward Earth. Airplane wings use **lift** and **thrust** to help overcome gravity and speed into the air.

Friction works against motion. It is created when two objects rub against each other. Friction slows things down.

FACT

Friction is useful in many ways. Car tires create friction to help a driver control the car. Car brakes use friction to reduce speed and allow vehicles to stop.

lift—the upward force that causes an object to rise into the air
thrust—the force that pushes a vehicle forward

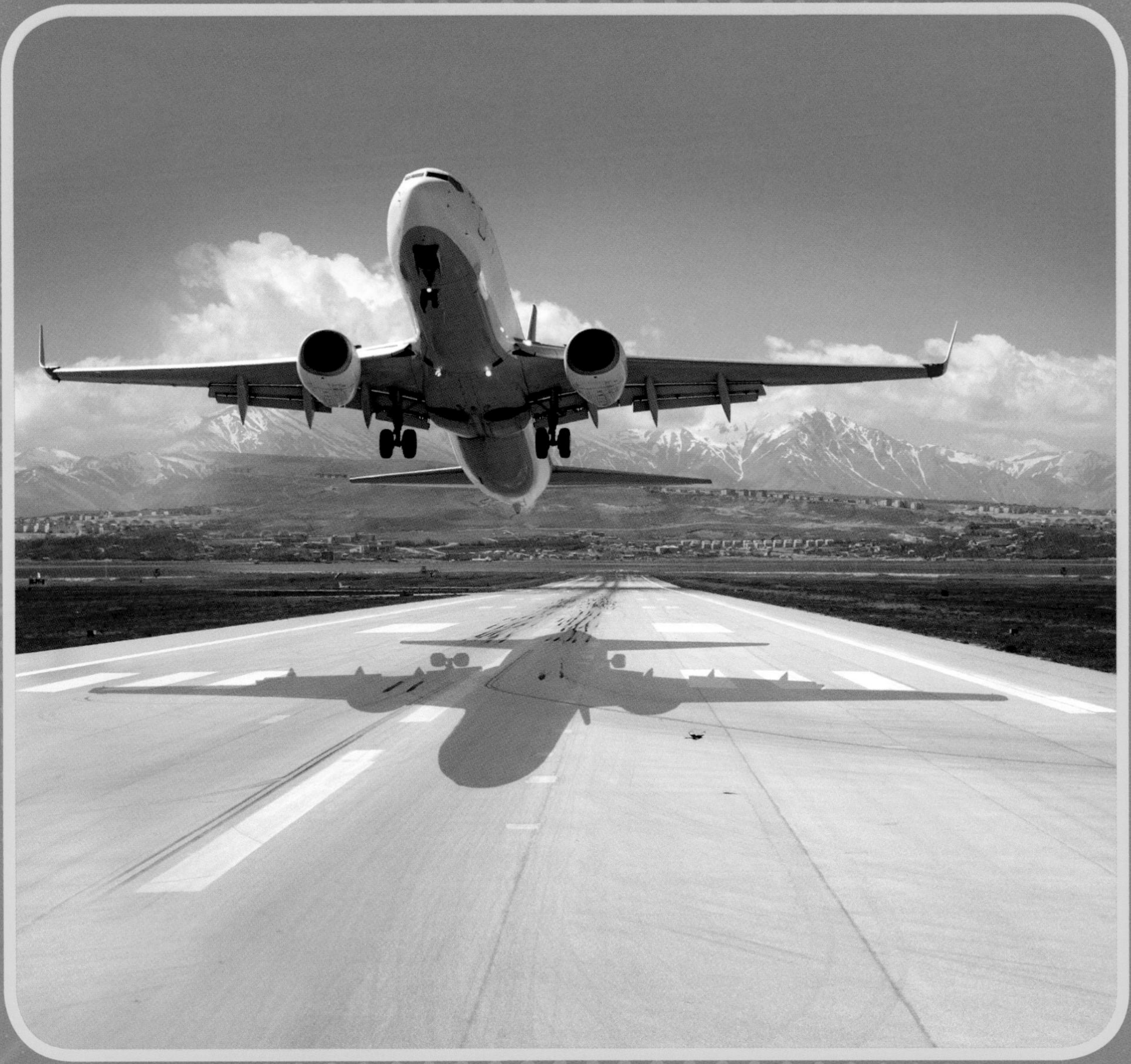

CHAPTER 2

FASTEST ANIMALS

Superman isn't alone when it comes to moving fast. Many animals also reach incredible speeds. Cheetahs are Earth's fastest running animals. A cheetah can accelerate from zero to 60 miles (97 km) per hour in just three seconds!

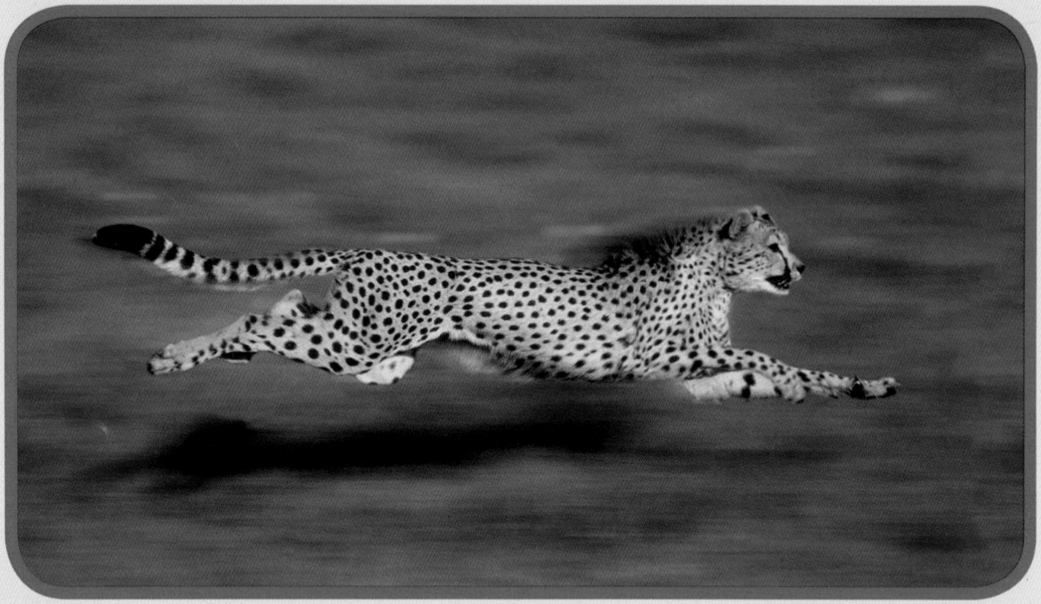

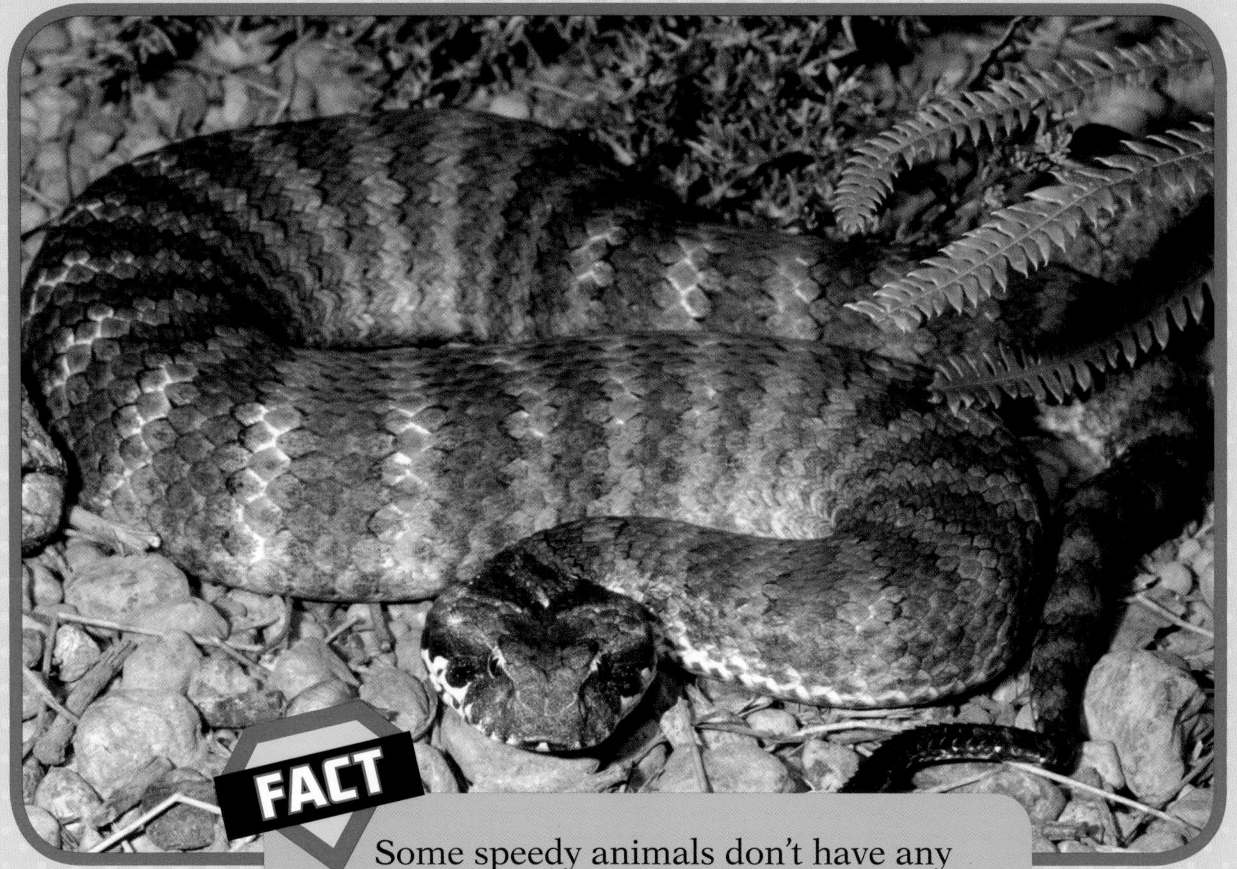

FACT

Some speedy animals don't have any legs. Australia's death adder is one of the fastest snakes in the world. It can strike victims in under 0.15 seconds!

When diving to catch **prey**, the peregrine falcon can travel up to 200 miles (322 km) per hour. Anna's hummingbirds can move 385 body lengths per second. This quick movement makes the hummingbird the fastest animal on Earth!

peregrine falcon

FACT

Mosquitoes beat their wings 500 times every second.

prey—an animal hunted by another animal for food

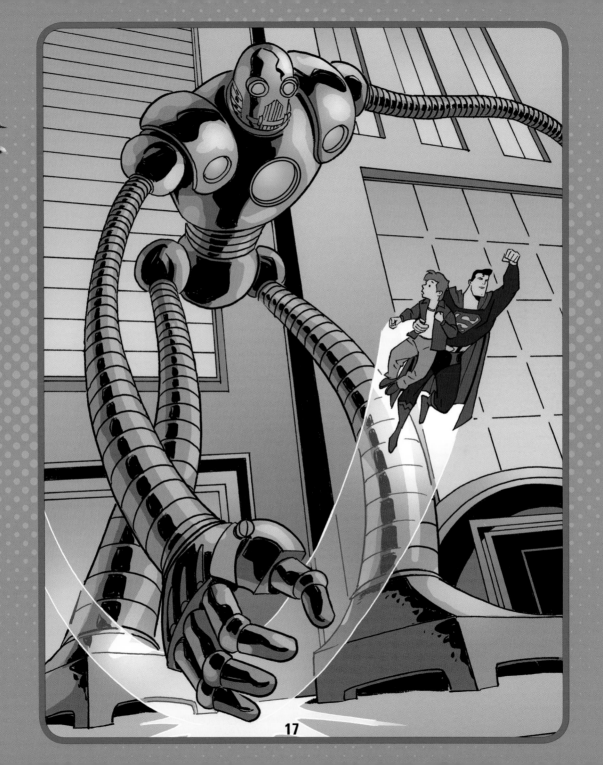

17

CHAPTER 3

SPEEDIEST VEHICLES

Superman doesn't need a vehicle to travel fast. But **engineers** continually test the limits of speed. Supercars are the fastest cars on the road today. In 2014, the Hennessey Venom GT accelerated from zero to 200 miles (322 km) per hour in just 20.3 seconds. The supercar topped out at 270 miles (435 km) per hour.

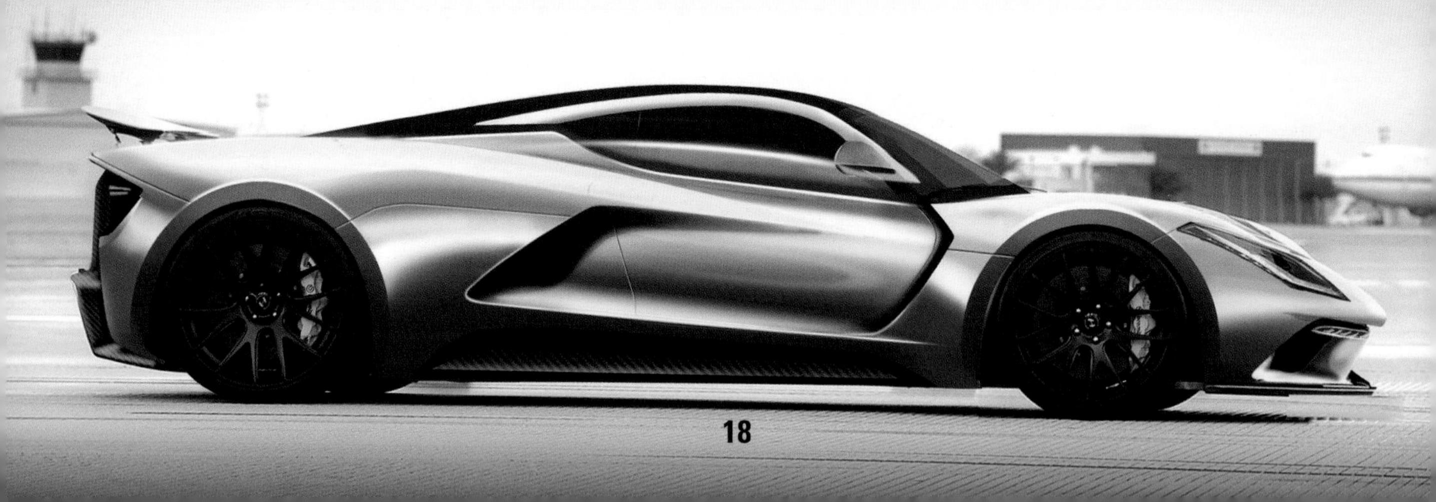

Art Arfons
GREEN MONSTER
Firestone
STP
Ed Snyder

FACT

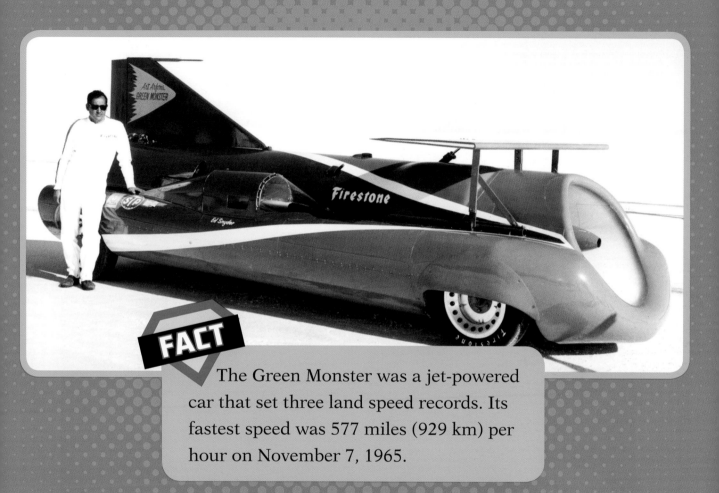

The Green Monster was a jet-powered car that set three land speed records. Its fastest speed was 577 miles (929 km) per hour on November 7, 1965.

engineer—a person who uses science and math to plan, design, or build

To mimic Superman's speed, people need to take to the air. The SR-71 Blackbird set a speed record of 2,193 miles (3,529 km) per hour in 1976. The X-15 rocket aircraft went even faster. It set a speed record of 4,520 miles (7,270 km) per hour.

FACT

In 2016, the *Juno* spacecraft became the fastest man-made vehicle. It traveled more than 165,000 miles (265,500 km) per hour as it approached Jupiter.

READ THEM ALL!

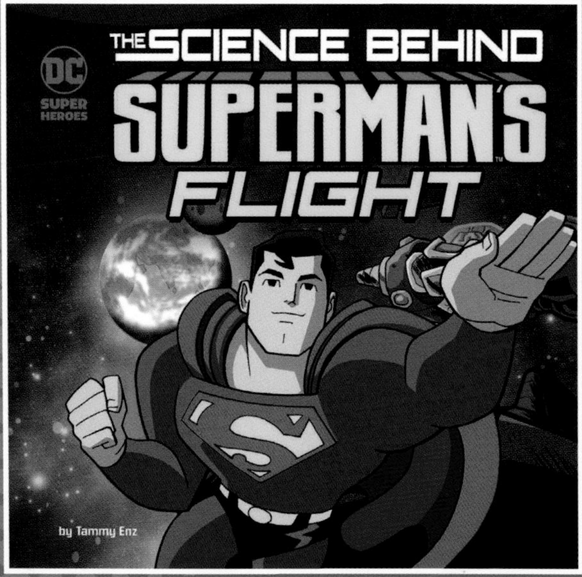
THE SCIENCE BEHIND
SUPERMAN'S
FLIGHT
DC SUPER HEROES
by Tammy Enz

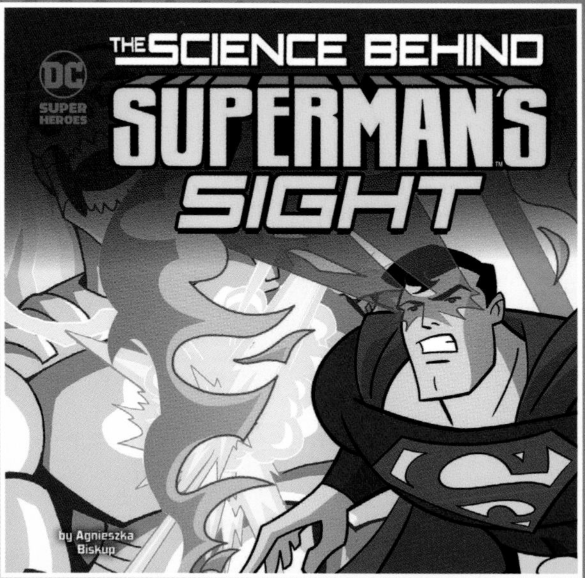
THE SCIENCE BEHIND
SUPERMAN'S
SIGHT
DC SUPER HEROES
by Agnieszka Biskup

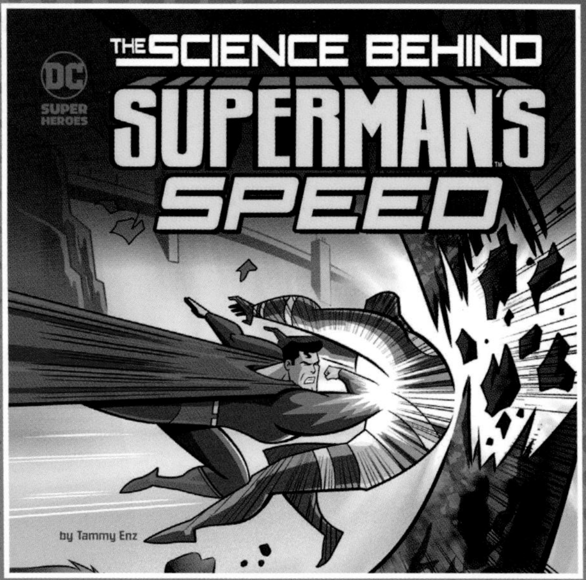
THE SCIENCE BEHIND
SUPERMAN'S
SPEED
DC SUPER HEROES
by Tammy Enz

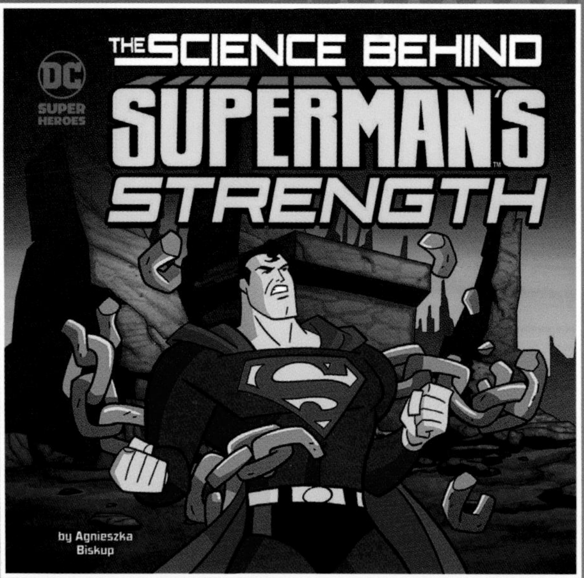
THE SCIENCE BEHIND
SUPERMAN'S
STRENGTH
DC SUPER HEROES
by Agnieszka Biskup

READ MORE

Enz, Tammy. *The Science Behind Batman's Ground Vehicles.* Science Behind Batman. North Mankato, Minn.: Capstone Press, 2016.

Farndon, John. *Megafast Planes.* Megafast. Minneapolis: Hungry Tomato, 2016.

Polydoros, Lori. *Drag Racing.* Super Speed. North Mankato, Minn.: Capstone Press, 2013.

INTERNET SITES

FactHound offers a safe, fun way to find Internet sites related to this book. All of the sites on FactHound have been researched by our staff.

Here's all you do:
Visit *www.facthound.com*
Type in this code: 9781515750963

INDEX

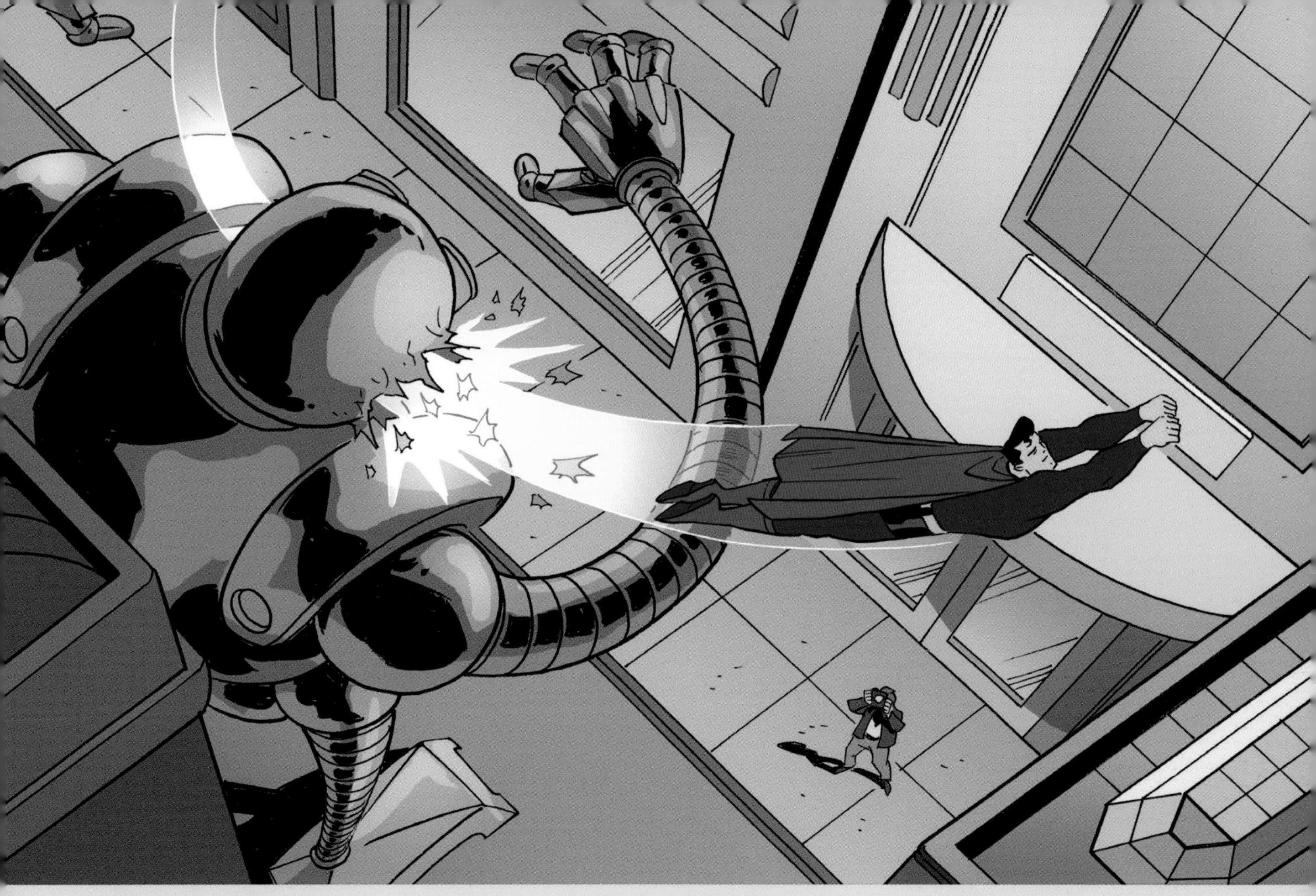

Superman's power of speed is beyond the ability of human beings. But it reminds us that speed is all around us. With the science of speed, people are finding ways to travel faster every day.

GLOSSARY

acceleration (ak-sel-uh-RAY-shuhn)—rate of change of the velocity of a moving object

engineer (en-juh-NEER)—a person who uses science and math to plan, design, or build

lift (LIFT)—the upward force of air that causes an object to fly

orbit (OR-bit)—to travel around an object in space

prey (PRAY)—an animal hunted by another animal for food

sound wave (SOUND WAYV)—a wave or vibration that travels through a substance, such as air

thrust (THRUHST)—the force that pushes a vehicle forward

velocity (vuh-LOSS-uh-tee)—a measurement of both the speed and direction an object is moving

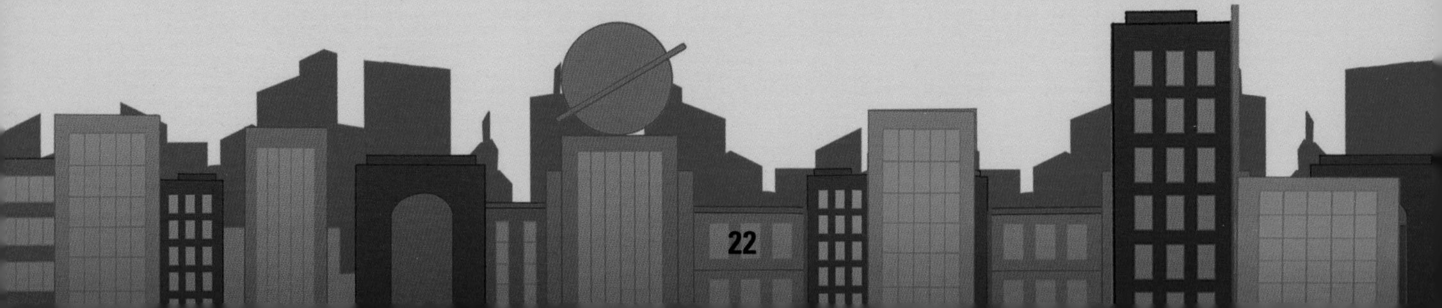